W9-BRV-267

QUALITY CUSTOMER SERVICE

THIRD EDITION

William B. Martin, Ph.D.

A FIFTY MINUTE™ SERIES BOOK

CRISP PUBLICATIONS, INC.
Menlo Park, California

QUALITY CUSTOMER SERVICE

THIRD EDITION

William B. Martin, Ph.D.

CREDITS
Editor: **Michael Crisp**
Typesetting: **Interface Studio**
Cover Design: **Carol Harris**
Artwork: **Ralph Mapson**

The cartoon on the cover has been reprinted by permission of the author Sidney Harris and is from the book, "WHAT'S SO FUNNY ABOUT BUSINESS?", ©1986 William Kaufmann, Inc., 1990 Crisp Publications, Inc., 1200 Hamilton Court, Menlo Park, CA 94025.

English language Crisp books are distributed worldwide. Our major international distributors include:

CANADA: Reid Publishing Ltd., Box 69559—109 Thomas St., Oakville, Ontario Canada L6J 7R4. TEL: (416) 842-4428, FAX: (416) 842-9327

AUSTRALIA: Career Builders, P. O. Box 1051, Springwood, Brisbane, Queensland, Australia 4127. TEL: 841-1061, FAX: 841-1580

NEW ZEALAND: Career Builders, P. O. Box 571, Manurewa, Auckland, New Zealand. TEL: 266-5276, FAX: 266-4152

JAPAN: Phoenix Associates Co., Mizuho Bldg. 2-12-2, Kami Osaki, Shinagawa-Ku, Tokyo 141, Japan. TEL: 3-443-7231, FAX: 3-443-7640

Selected Crisp titles are also available in other languages. Contact International Rights Manager Tim Polk at (800) 442-7477 for more information.

Library of Congress Catalog Card Number 92-082933
Martin, William
Quality Customer Service: Third Edition
ISBN 1-56052-203-8

This book is printed on recyclable paper with soy ink.

PRINTED WITH SOY INK

ABOUT THIS BOOK

This book is for people who currently work, or plan to work, in a job that requires interaction with customers from outside of the organization as well as inside. It is addressed to the front-line employee who ultimately determines the quality level of customer service. The material was designed to make sure that all points of customer contact—those ''moments of truth''—occur in the best way possible. In short, this book may be used by an organization that wants to teach employees how to provide quality customer service.

The premise of this book is twofold: 1) quality customer service is the key to success for any employee with customer service responsibility, and 2) quality customer service is the foundation upon which an organization's success and profits are built.

Unfortunately, a majority of organizations today concentrate on the technical side of job performance and devote far too little time to the ''people side'' of business. Training is often catch-as-catch-can because of limited resources, busy schedules and a lack of time. Also many service supervisors are not experienced enough to properly train employees in effective customer relation skills.

This program is useful for training new employees as well as promoting the continued development of more experienced personnel. All that is required is an interested employee, a pencil, and some time. Using *Quality Customer Service* and follow-up on the part of the manager or trainer will provide measurably improved customer service for any organization.

i

QUALITY CUSTOMER SERVICE: Third Edition

IS THIS BOOK FOR YOU?

This book is for YOU if your job requires you to interact with other people. The people with whom you may interact fall into two groups: (1) **internal** and (2) **external**.

IF YOU PROVIDE SERVICE TO EITHER ONE OR BOTH OF THESE GROUPS, THEY ARE YOUR CUSTOMERS.

INTERNAL CUSTOMERS are people inside of your organization who **depend on you for service.**

EXTERNAL CUSTOMERS are people outside of your organization who **depend on you for service.**

Common names used to describe INTERNAL customers

- the accounting department
- my boss
- co-workers
- engineering
- the people in operations
- the marketing group
- the production crew
- those guys on the third floor
- the people down the hall

Common names used to describe EXTERNAL customers

- customers
- clients
- patients
- guests
- students
- constituents
- stakeholders

WHO ARE YOUR CUSTOMERS? WHAT DO YOU CALL THEM?

Name some of your INTERNAL customers here.
(They may be individuals, groups, departments and/or allied organizations.)

Name some of your EXTERNAL customers here.
(They may be individuals, groups or entire organizations.)

TO THE READER

The person who gave you this book wants you to read it carefully, working all of the exercises and activities. If you have any problems as you proceed, ask your trainer/supervisor for assistance.

Once you have read the book, and completed its exercises, you will be better prepared to practice the secrets of quality customer service. What you learn, and the subsequent changes this program brings, are far more important than the time it takes to finish. Read slowly and think about each point as it is introduced because it is there for you.

Interacting with customers should be fun and challenging. Ideally, you should enjoy interacting with the people with whom your job brings you in contact.

Dealing effectively with people requires many principles, methods and skills which need to be recognized, learned and practiced. Therefore, the way to make the most of your job is to enjoy it as fully as possible and learn all you can about the process. It is the combination of your attitude and your skills that will determine the kind of customer service you provide for your employer. *Quality Customer Service* can help make you a winner!

Good Luck!

William B. Martin

William B. Martin

P.S. It is a good idea to keep *Quality Customer Service* handy throughout your training as you may wish to refer to it for review.

CONTENTS

CONTENTS (continued)

P A R T

I

Do You Have What It Takes To Provide Outstanding Quality Customer Service?

DO YOU HAVE WHAT IT TAKES TO PROVIDE OUTSTANDING CUSTOMER SERVICE?

The people in your organization think so, or they wouldn't have hired you.

NOW IS THE TIME TO PROVE THEM CORRECT.

MAKE YOUR CHOICE NOW

SERVICE SUCCESSES	SERVICE FAILURES
Those with a positive attitude and cheerful outlook	Those who seem depressed or angry
Those who genuinely enjoy working with and for other people	Those who would rather work alone or with ''things''
Those with the ability to put the customer on ''center stage'' rather than themselves	Those who need to be the center of attention
Those with a high energy level and who enjoy a fast pace	Those who work at their own relaxed pace
Those who view their job primarily as a human relations profession	Those who consider technical aspects of the job more important than customer satisfaction
Those who are flexible and enjoy new demands and experiences	Those who must have things happen in an orderly and predictable way
Those who can allow customers to be right (even on those occasions when they are not)	Those who need others to know that they are right

Add your own:

_____

_____

_____

Add your own:

_____

_____

_____

Differences between effective and ineffective service is a matter of sensitivity, sincerity, attitude and human relations skills — all of which can be learned.

It isn't enough to simply perform the duties of your job. YOU MUST ALSO HAVE THE RIGHT APPROACH.

- A patient in a doctor's office wants more than a treatment.
- Airline passengers want more than a safe flight.
- Clients in a transaction want more than a settlement.
- Customers in a store want more than a product.
- Guests in hotels want more than a room.
- Restaurant patrons want more than a meal.
- Rental car customers want more than a car.

CUSTOMERS WANT MORE THAN JUST THE PRODUCT OR SERVICE THAT IS OFFERED. THEY ALSO WANT TO BE TREATED WELL!

HOW GOOD ARE YOUR SERVICE SKILLS?

DO YOU HAVE THE RIGHT STUFF?

Remember:
Quality Customer Service providers are made, not born.

CUSTOMER RELATIONS POTENTIAL SCALE

I control my moods most of the time.	10 9 8 7 6 5 4 3 2 1	I have limited control over my moods.
It is possible for me to be pleasant to people who are indifferent to me.	10 9 8 7 6 5 4 3 2 1	I simply can't be pleasant if people are not nice to me.
I like most people and enjoy meeting with others.	10 9 8 7 6 5 4 3 2 1	I have difficulties getting along with others.
I enjoy being of service to others.	10 9 8 7 6 5 4 3 2 1	People should help themselves.
I do not mind apologizing for mistakes even if I did not make them.	10 9 8 7 6 5 4 3 2 1	Apologizing for a mistake I didn't make is wrong.
I take pride in my ability to communicate verbally with others.	10 9 8 7 6 5 4 3 2 1	I would rather interact with others in writing.
I'm good at remembering names and faces, and make efforts to improve this skill when meeting others.	10 9 8 7 6 5 4 3 2 1	Why bother remembering a name or face if you will never see that person again?
Smiling comes naturally for me.	10 9 8 7 6 5 4 3 2 1	I am more serious by nature.
I like seeing others enjoy themselves.	10 9 8 7 6 5 4 3 2 1	I have no motivation to please others, especially those I don't know.
I keep myself clean and well groomed.	10 9 8 7 6 5 4 3 2 1	Being clean and well groomed is not all that important.

TOTAL SCORE _____

If you rated yourself 80 or above, you are probably excellent with customers, clients or guests. If you rated yourself between 50 and 80, you may need to learn better human relations skills before working with the public. If you scored under 50, working with customers is probably a poor career choice for you.

WHAT IS QUALITY CUSTOMER SERVICE?

Two primary dimensions make up quality customer service: the *procedural* dimension and *personal* dimension. Each is critical to the delivery of QUALITY service.

THE PROCEDURAL SIDE of service consists of the established systems and procedures to deliver products and/or service.

THE PERSONAL SIDE of service is how service personnel, (using their attitudes, behaviors and verbal skills) interact with customers.

The exercises and activities in this book reflect both dimensions of QUALITY SERVICE.

QUALITY SERVICE EXERCISE

The diagrams below show the procedural and personal dimensions in graphic form.

The vertical axis represents the degree of procedural service and the horizontal axis reflects a measure of personal service.

Study each diagram below. HOW WOULD YOU DESCRIBE THE NATURE OF THE SERVICE REFLECTED IN EACH DIAGRAM? Indicate your responses in the spaces provided.

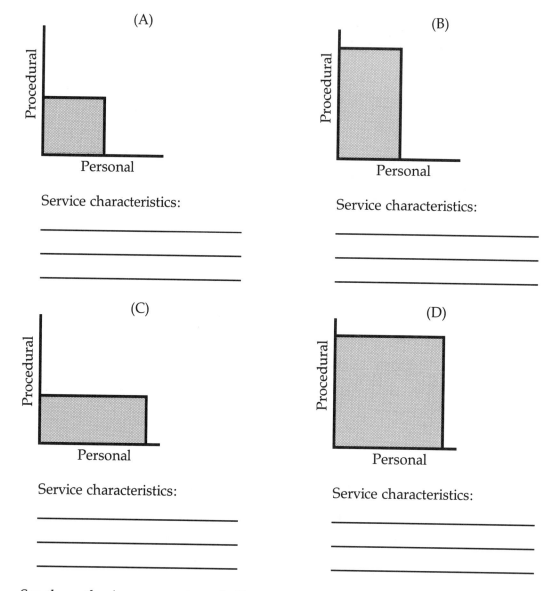

(A)

Service characteristics:

_____

_____

_____

(B)

Service characteristics:

_____

_____

_____

(C)

Service characteristics:

_____

_____

_____

(D)

Service characteristics:

_____

_____

_____

See the author's response to each diagram on the next page.

FOUR TYPES OF SERVICE

Diagram A:
The Freezer

This reflects an operation that is low in both personal and procedural service. This "freezer" approach to service communicates to customers, "We don't care."

Diagram B:
The Factory

This diagram represents proficient procedural service but a weakness in the personal dimension. This "factory" approach to service communicates to customers, "You are a number. We are here to process you."

Diagram C:
The Friendly Zoo

The "friendly zoo" approach to service is very personal but lacks procedural consistency. This type of service communicates to customers, "We are trying hard, but don't really know what we're doing."

Diagram D:
Q.C.S.

This diagram represents QUALITY CUSTOMER SERVICE. It is strong in both the personal and procedural dimensions. It communicates to members, "We care and we deliver."

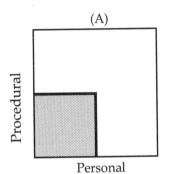

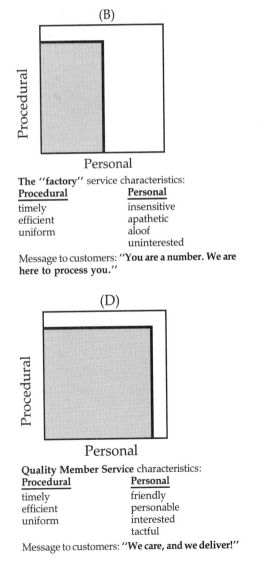

(A) Procedural / Personal

The "freezer" service characteristics:

Procedural	Personal
slow	insensitive
inconsistent	cold or impersonal
disorganized	apathetic
chaotic	aloof
inconvenient	uninterested

Message to customers: **"We don't care."**

(B) Procedural / Personal

The "factory" service characteristics:

Procedural	Personal
timely	insensitive
efficient	apathetic
uniform	aloof
	uninterested

Message to customers: **"You are a number. We are here to process you."**

(C) Procedural / Personal

The "friendly zoo" service characteristics:

Procedural	Personal
slow	friendly
inconsistent	personable
disorganized	interested
chaotic	tactful

Message to customers: **"We are trying hard, but we don't really know what we're doing."**

(D) Procedural / Personal

Quality Member Service characteristics:

Procedural	Personal
timely	friendly
efficient	personable
uniform	interested
	tactful

Message to customers: **"We care, and we deliver!"**

FOUR REASONS WHY QUALITY SERVICE IS IMPORTANT

1. Growth of the service industry

There are more businesses providing services than ever before. Almost half of U.S. businesses are service related and employ approximately one-third of the total workforce. The growth of service related organizations continues to expand.

2. Increased competition

Whether it's the corner gas station, Joe's Plumbing Service, a giant retail outlet, or an international bank; competition is keen. Business survival depends on obtaining the competitive edge. Quality customer service provides the competitive advantage for thousands of organizations.

3. Greater understanding of consumers

We know more today than ever before about why customers patronize certain services and avoid others. Quality products, along with a realistic price, are a must; but that's not all. Customers also want to be treated well and do repeat business with places that emphasize service.

4. Quality customer service makes economic sense.

The lifeblood of any company is repeat business. Expanding the customer base is vital. This means companies not only have to attract new clients or customers, but also must keep existing ones. Quality customer service helps make this happen.

Following is a partial list of organizations that benefit from "quality customer service."

Hotels	Travel and tour related businesses
Banks	Clubs
Restaurants	Supermarkets
Department stores	Service and repair companies
Retail outlets	Health facilities
Hospitals	Utility companies
Insurance companies	Federal and state agencies
Libraries	Finance and brokerage businesses
Doctors' offices	Lawyers' offices
Universities	Police departments
Security services	Construction companies

Is your type of organization represented above?

Should it be?

QUALITY CUSTOMER SERVICE

may be
important
to my
organization

BUT,

WHAT WILL IT DO
FOR ME?

WHY SUCCESS IN CUSTOMER RELATIONS IS IMPORTANT TO YOU

Common sense should tell you that the success you have with customers will increase the amount of money you make, whether in salary increases or tips, as well as make you more promotable. Money aside, success in customer relations also provides many PERSONAL benefits.

Read each statement below. Determine which are *true* and which are *false* about the benefits good customer relations skills can bring to you.

(Check your answers with those of the author at the bottom of the page.)

True or False

_____ 1. Working with customers is usually more enjoyable than working at a routine technical job.

_____ 2. Improving interpersonal skills can help develop a personality.

_____ 3. The ability to provide the best possible customer service is a continuous challenge that keeps a job interesting.

_____ 4. Most top executives lack effective customer relations skills.

_____ 5. Ongoing success with customers can lead to better job security and opportunity for promotion.

_____ 6. Learning to treat customers as special people has a ''carry over'' value to future jobs.

_____ 7. What you learn about customer/client services in an entry level position is often more important than the money you make.

_____ 8. Service jobs where you meet the public are easier than most technical jobs.

_____ 9. Skill in performing the mechanics of your job is more important than your attitude about how you perform it.

_____ 10. Smiles are contagious.

ANSWERS: 1. T 2. T 3. T 4. F (Many top executives use effective guest relations skills to get them to the top.) 5. T 6. T 7. T 8. F (Guest relations jobs are more demanding because they require you to stay positive all the time.) 9. F (Your attitude is at least as important as your job skills.) 10. T

QUALITY CUSTOMER SERVICE

Treating customers professionally is like playing a game such as baseball or softball.

1. Like a ballgame, it is sometimes possible to do everything right and still not win.

2. But, your CUSTOMER SERVICE BATTING AVERAGE will increase when you *cover the bases the right way.*

   and

3. When customers, clients and/or guests RETURN because they have been treated well, you know you have SCORED.

14

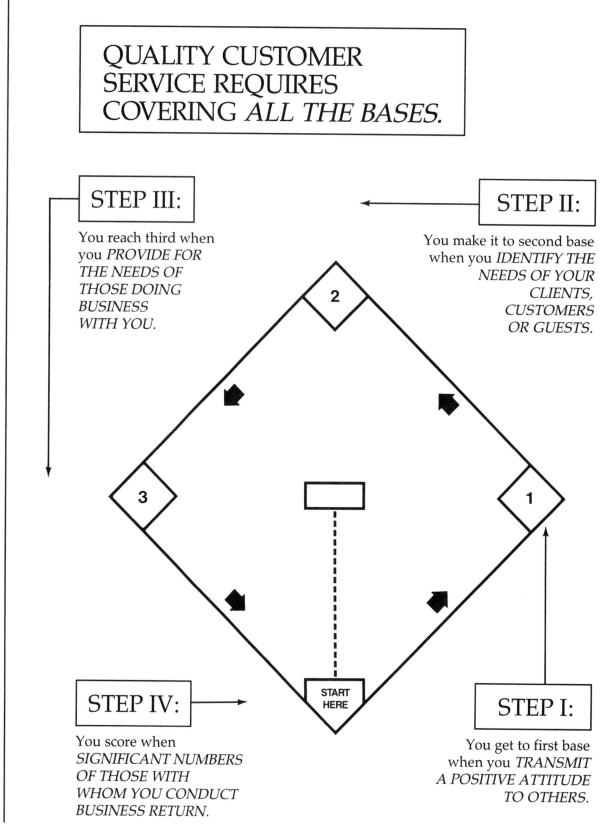

QUALITY CUSTOMER SERVICE REQUIRES COVERING *ALL THE BASES.*

STEP III:

You reach third when you *PROVIDE FOR THE NEEDS OF THOSE DOING BUSINESS WITH YOU.*

STEP II:

You make it to second base when you *IDENTIFY THE NEEDS OF YOUR CLIENTS, CUSTOMERS OR GUESTS.*

2

3

1

START HERE

STEP IV:

You score when *SIGNIFICANT NUMBERS OF THOSE WITH WHOM YOU CONDUCT BUSINESS RETURN.*

STEP I:

You get to first base when you *TRANSMIT A POSITIVE ATTITUDE TO OTHERS.*

PART

II

Four Steps To
Quality
Customer Service

STEP I: SEND A POSITIVE ATTITUDE TO OTHERS

ATTITUDE:

1. An attitude is a state of mind influenced by feelings, thought and action tendencies.

2. The attitude you send out is usually the attitude you get back.

SEND A POSITIVE ATTITUDE TO OTHERS

Alison was a disagreeable sort. Her fellow workers at the supermarket where she was a checker found her moody. Customers did not appreciate her sour disposition, and a few said so to the manager. When business took a temporary downswing, it came as no surprise when Alison was the first to be laid off.

RATE YOURSELF

HOW POSITIVE IS YOUR ATTITUDE?

Most customer service employees that fail do so because of ATTITUDE. If you don't get to first base with customers, clients or guests, the game is over before it begins.

Nothing in customer service is better than SENDING A POSITIVE ATTITUDE to all with whom you come in contact.

The attitude you project to others depends primarily on the way you look at your job. To measure your attitude toward others complete this exercise.

CIRCLE THE EXTENT YOU AGREE OR DISAGREE WITH EACH STATEMENT.

	Agree			Disagree	
1. There is nothing demeaning about assisting or serving others.	5	4	3	2	1
2. I can be cheerful and positive to everyone regardless of age or appearance.	5	4	3	2	1
3. On bad days when nothing goes right, I can still find ways to be positive.	5	4	3	2	1
4. The higher the quality of service I provide during work, the better I feel.	5	4	3	2	1
5. I am enthusiastic about my job.	5	4	3	2	1
6. Encountering difficult "people" situations from time to time will not cause me to be negative.	5	4	3	2	1
7. The idea of being a professional at customer contact is motivating.	5	4	3	2	1
8. Performing a "people-oriented" job is both challenging and fun.	5	4	3	2	1
9. I receive great pleasure when others compliment me or my organization for superior service.	5	4	3	2	1
10. Doing well in all aspects of my job is very important to me.	5	4	3	2	1

TOTAL SCORE _____

If you scored above 40, you have an excellent attitude toward your job. If you scored between 25 and 40, you seem to have some reservations that should be examined before you make a career which involves customer contact. A rating below 25 indicates a non-customer relations job would probably be best for you.

QUALITY CUSTOMER SERVICE: Third Edition

STEP I: ONE GOOD WAY
TO SEND A
POSITIVE ATTITUDE
IS BY . . .

YOUR APPEARANCE

You never get a *second* chance to create a positive *first* impression.

FIRST IMPRESSIONS ARE CRITICAL BECAUSE THERE MAY BE NO OPPORTUNITY FOR A SECOND IMPRESSION!

COMMUNICATING YOUR BEST IMAGE

Like an actor or actress, interacting with others requires you to be on stage at all times. Creating a good first impression is essential. It is also important to understand that there is a direct connection between how you look to yourself and your attitude. The better your self-image when you encounter customers, clients or guests, the more positive you will be.

Rate yourself on each grooming area presented below. If you circle a ''5'' you are saying that improvement is not required. If you circle a ''1,'' or ''2,'' you need considerable improvement. Be honest.

	Excellent	Good	Fair	Weak	Poor
Hairstyle, hair grooming (appropriate length & cleanliness)	5	4	3	2	1
Personal habits of cleanliness (body)	5	4	3	2	1
Personal habits of cleanliness (hands, fingernails and teeth)	5	4	3	2	1
Clothing and jewelry (appropriate to the situation)	5	4	3	2	1
Neatness (shoes shined, clothes clean, well pressed, etc.)	5	4	3	2	1
General grooming: Will your appearance reflect professionalism on the job?	5	4	3	2	1

WHEN IT COMES TO APPEARANCE ON THE JOB, I WOULD RATE MYSELF:

☐ EXCELLENT   ☐ GOOD   ☐ NEED IMPROVEMENT

> THE MOST SUCCESSFUL PEOPLE IN CUSTOMER CONTACT JOBS CLAIM THAT TO BE SHARP MENTALLY MEANS COMMUNICATING A POSITIVE SELF-IMAGE.

STEP I: SEND A POSITIVE ATTITUDE BY YOUR

BODY LANGUAGE

Did you know that body language can account for more than half of the message you communicate?

Here is a body language checklist. Place a check in the square if you can answer "yes" to the question.

☐ Do you hold your head high and steady?

☐ Do your arms move in a natural, unaffected manner?

☐ Are your facial muscles relaxed and under control?

☐ Do you find it easy to maintain a natural smile?

☐ Is your body movement controlled, neither harried nor too casual?

☐ Do you find it easy to maintain eye contact with people you are talking to?

BODY LANGUAGE EXERCISE

Four sets of opposite nonverbal messages are presented below.

CAN YOU DESCRIBE THE POSSIBLE MESSAGES THESE FORMS OF
BODY LANGUAGE SEND TO GUESTS?

<u>POSITIVE MESSAGES</u>

Face is relaxed and under control.

This communicates _____
_____
_____

Smile is natural and comfortable.

This communicates _____
_____
_____

Eye contact is maintained when
talking and listening to others.

This communicates _____
_____
_____

Body movement is relaxed, yet
deliberate and controlled.

This communicates _____
_____
_____

<u>NEGATIVE MESSAGES</u>

Face is anxious and uptight.

This communicates _____
_____
_____

Smile is missing or forced.

This communicates _____
_____
_____

Eye contact is avoided when
talking and listening.

This communicates _____
_____
_____

Body movement is harried and
rushed.

This communicates _____
_____
_____

Compare your comments with those of the author on page 85.

STEP 1: SEND A POSITIVE ATTITUDE BY ...

THE SOUND OF YOUR VOICE

THE TONE OF YOUR VOICE, OR *HOW* YOU SAY SOMETHING, IS OFTEN MORE IMPORTANT THAN THE WORDS YOU USE.

Charley is a ten year veteran on the local police force. As a patrolman in one of the toughest parts of town, he developed an authoritarian and intimidating tone to his voice. Now that Charley has been transferred to community affairs, he has had to learn to adjust his voice to project a more conciliatory and friendly image.

LISTENING TO THE SOUND OF YOUR OWN VOICE

The tone of voice you use with others may mean the difference between:

(1) acceptable job success and GREAT job success, and

(2) adequate customer service and QUALITY customer service.

Below are different voice styles by which people communicate. Which seem to best describe yours? Check the one(s) with which you identify most.

_____ My voice becomes agitated and/or loud when I am angry.

_____ I speak more quickly when nervous.

_____ My voice slows significantly and/or becomes quieter when I get tired.

_____ Others describe my tone of voice as ''upbeat.''

_____ Friends regard my tone of voice as warm and understanding when we are in a serious conversation.

_____ I can control my tone of voice in most situations.

_____ My voice can sound authoritarian and demanding when required.

_____ Others consider my voice meek.

_____ I'm lucky because my voice is clear, direct and natural.

_____ My vocabulary and style of speaking tends to be serious and scholarly.

Some of the above are better than others when interacting with customers. Please review the comments of the author on page 85.

Note: This may be a difficult exercise for those not accustomed to listening to themselves. Ask a friend to help you complete this exercise; it may provide some invaluable insights. Use of a tape recorder or telephone answering device can also be helpful.

26

STEP I: SEND A POSITIVE ATTITUDE WHEN USING THE

TELEPHONE

Skill on the telephone is important because . . .

(1) You have only your voice to rely on. Body language, written messages and visual aids are unavailable.

(2) When you are on the phone with a customer or client, YOU ARE *THE* SINGLE representative of your company. In other words, YOU ARE YOUR ORGANIZATION.

QUESTION: True or False? When you answer the phone with a smile on your face, the tone of your voice will communicate a positive attitude to the person calling you.

ANSWER: True

TELEPHONE QUIZ

Treating customers professionally means being as pleasant over the phone as you are in person. Take the telephone quiz below and see if you can score 100 percent.

True or False

_____ 1. It is okay to keep someone waiting on the phone while you attend to another equally important task.

_____ 2. You should actually smile when you answer the telephone.

_____ 3. If nobody is around to answer a ringing phone and it is not your assigned job, the best thing to do is let it ring.

_____ 4. It is acceptable to not return a call. If the call was important, the calling party will try again.

_____ 5. If a customer is rude, it is your right to be equally snippy.

_____ 6. You should identify yourself by name when answering a business related telephone call.

_____ 7. If business is slow, it is perfectly acceptable to make personal calls to your friends.

_____ 8. It is important to communicate a sincere interest in the caller and the information that is being requested or provided.

_____ 9. The conversation should be ended in an upbeat manner, with a summary of any action to be taken.

_____ 10. When you are upset, it is possible to communicate a negative attitude over the phone without realizing it.

ANSWERS: 1) F 2) T 3) F 4) F 5) F 6) T 7) F 8) T 9) T 10) T

28

STEP I: SEND A POSITIVE
ATTITUDE BY . . .

STAYING ENERGIZED

Three customer-service MYTHS:

1. Customer service is less tiring than other jobs that require hard physical labor.

2. Providing QUALITY customer service every day–all the time–is easy.

3. If you can be helpful and friendly to one customer, then you will find it just as easy to treat hundreds of customers the same way.

Customer-service REALITIES:

1. Customer service requires the exertion of EMOTIONAL LABOR. Emotional labor takes its toll on your energy level just like physical labor does; that is, it makes you tired.

2. The ideas and concepts presented in this book are simple to understand. But that does not mean that they are necessarily easy to accomplish every day all the time. Providing quality customer service on a regular basis can be very challenging.

3. Serving many customers over an extended period of time can be very tiring. When you have exhausted your reservoir of emotional energy, it is called CONTACT OVERLOAD SYNDROME.

   When you are suffering from contact overload syndrome you can become –

   - tired
   - listless
   - dejected
   - grouchy/impatient
   - even clumsy

Each one of these conditions REDUCES your ability to provide QUALITY CUSTOMER SERVICE.

IS CONTACT OVERLOAD SYNDROME A POTENTIAL PROBLEM FOR YOU?

If so, how?

_____

_____

_____

_____

_____

_____

When you are EMOTIONALLY TIRED, what can you do to RE-ENERGIZE YOURSELF?

_____

_____

_____

_____

_____

_____

Still going . . . but for how long?

We all need our batteries charged from time to time!

Your ability to re-energize yourself is important to maintaining a positive attitude toward your customers.

Maintaining your POSITIVE ATTITUDE is your KEY to delivering QUALITY CUSTOMER SERVICE every minute on the job.

WHY SEND A POSITIVE ATTITUDE?

I. *Customer relations is an integral part of your job —
not an extension of it.*

Nothing is more important to your company than customers.
Without them, your company could not exist.

II. *Satisfied customers are essential to the success of your
organization.*

Business grows through satisfied customers. Satisfied
customers not only come back, but they also bring
their friends.

III. *Quality customer care is learned not inherited.*

Like mastering any skill, being able to excel in customer care
requires practice and experience. The more you put into it,
the more you will receive from it.

CASE #1

"In other companies where I have worked, the maintenance
departments made me feel guilty about calling them for
help. But here, the people in maintenance are a joy to
work with. No matter what time of day or night, no
matter what the problem is, they are always smiling and
willing to help. That sure makes my job a lot easier."
                                                    Office Worker

CASE #1
CUSTOMER CONTACT

Situation—Thelma's Performance Appraisal

Thelma works in a fast-food restaurant as a counter person. Here is what Thelma's manager had to say on her last performance appraisal.

"Thelma is extremely conscientious about getting her work done. She follows the outlined procedures exactly. She can be relied upon to get a job done quickly and efficiently. She often works overtime and does so without complaining. She is a hard worker who strives to do the technical part of her job right, and is highly productive.

However, when it comes to interacting with customers, Thelma needs considerable improvement. She often fails to see their point of view or consider their feelings. She sometimes acts like customers are an irritation interrupting her work. She is regarded by some as uncaring and tends to be inflexible when they request extra service.

If her performance continues, it will be necessary to reposition Thelma to the laundry where customer contact is limited."

QUESTIONS:	ANSWERS:

1. Is Thelma a good employee? Explain.

_____

_____

_____

2. Is the manager justified in his recommendations? Why or why not?

_____

_____

_____

3. What suggestions would you make to Thelma?

_____

_____

_____

(See the author's comments on page 85.)

STEP I:
SUMMARY AND FOLLOW-UP

SUMMARY

Reflecting a positive attitude on your job is nothing more than *really* liking your job and allowing your *actions and words* to broadcast this enjoyment to your customers, supervisors and fellow employees.

Positive attitudes are shown in your

☐ APPEARANCE
☐ BODY LANGUAGE
☐ THE SOUND OF YOUR VOICE, AND
☐ TELEPHONE SKILLS.

Make sure all of these reflect a positive attitude from you and check each one that still needs work on your part. Practice makes perfect.

FOLLOW-UP

You have now completed Step One of this program. This is a good time to sit down with your manager and/or trainer and talk about what you have learned. This is also a good time to clarify any questions you may have about the job.

TELL YOUR MANAGER YOU HAVE COMPLETED THIS SECTION AND ARRANGE A MEETING!

Use the space below to make notes about what you want to talk about and/or your questions.

THINGS TO DISCUSS

1) Questions to my manager about our customers.

2) Questions to co-workers about procedures and routines.

3) Some of "my ideas."

4) Follow-up based on discussion.

5) Other

STEP II: IDENTIFY THE NEEDS OF YOUR CUSTOMERS, GUESTS OR CLIENTS

Chain of command: The customer is the *boss.*

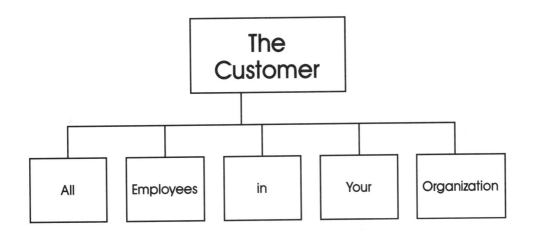

IT IS IMPORTANT FOR YOU TO KNOW . . .

- What your customers want
- What your customers need
- What your customers think
- What your customers feel
- Whether your customers are satisfied
- Whether your customers will return

HUMAN NEEDS

Following is a list of common human needs. Check those that reflect the needs of *your* customers/guests or clients.

☐   1.   The need to feel welcome.

☐   2.   The need for timely service.

☐   3.   The need to feel comfortable.

☐   4.   The need for orderly service.

☐   5.   The need to be understood.

☐   6.   The need to receive help or assistance.

☐   7.   The need to feel important.

☐   8.   The need to be appreciated.

☐   9.   The need to be recognized or remembered.

☐ 10.   The need for respect.

> Note: Give yourself a perfect score if you checked all 10 items.
> All customers, regardless of your business or operation, have these basic human needs to some degree or another.

STEP II: IDENTIFY CUSTOMER, GUEST, or CLIENT NEEDS BY...

Knowing the TIMING REQUIREMENTS For Quality Customer Service

Harry is sales manager at a large auto dealership. Since the dealer makes money from the service department, Harry plays a crucial role in the overall success of the company. One thing that Harry has done to build new business and convert it to repeat business is a new system to expedite the taking of service orders first thing in the morning. Since most customers drop their car off on the way to work, getting customers processed as quickly as possible is important. Meeting his customers' timing needs is just one way Harry has built his service department into the busiest one in the area.

TIMELINESS

HOW TIMELY SHOULD YOU BE?

Knowing the service time requirements for your operation is critical to performing quality service.

Five important personal contact points are listed below. There is also space for your manager/trainer to add additional items specific to your situation.

Indicate what you think the response time should be for each item. Then, ask your supervisor or trainer to do the same.

Once you have completed the exercise, try to arrange a meeting to discuss the timing needs of your job with your trainer or supervisor.

PERSONAL CONTACT POINT:

	Your Response:	Supervisor's Response:
1. A customer approaches the service area. He/She should be greeted, or have his/her presence acknowledged within _____ seconds.	_____	_____
2. Completing the initial paperwork or transaction should be completed within _____ minutes.	_____	_____
3. Any follow-up paperwork or transaction should be completed within _____ minutes.	_____	_____
4. Special requests should be handled within _____ or the guest, customer or client notified of the reason for the delay.	_____	_____
5. Telephone calls should be answered within _____ rings.	_____	_____
6. Other; specify _____	_____	_____

See comments of author on page 85.

A major university was experiencing declining student enrollments. Upon investigation of the problem, they discovered that they were taking much longer than other universities to respond to applications for admission. Prospective students were choosing to attend universities that responded in a more timely manner to their applications.

STEP II: ANTICIPATE CUSTOMER NEEDS BY...

Being *One Step Ahead* of Your Clients, Customers, Guests or Patients.

Bob and Ruth are nurses. They work for a different doctor at the same medical clinic. Before each day begins, Ruth goes over the appointment list and makes sure potentially needed supplies, equipment and medication are at her immediate disposal. Bob, on the other hand, attends to his patients' needs as they are treated. It is not surprising that Ruth finishes her patient load long before Bob.

ANTICIPATE THE NEEDS OF YOUR CUSTOMERS, CLIENTS OR GUESTS

Ask yourself: *"Have I considered all of the customer's needs?"*
"What will the guest need next?"
"How can I improve service now for my client?"

Then, offer or provide that service, ***WITHOUT REQUIRING A CUSTOMER TO ASK FOR IT!***

Five common service situations are listed below. After each, write in the space provided what you think is needed next.

After you complete the five specified situations, add five of your own, or ask your supervisor/trainer to add to the list.

SITUATION	ANTICIPATED NEED

1. A customer has waited longer than normal for service.

2. The client keeps glancing at his watch.

3. A woman guest with three small children approaches your service area.

4. Lines for your service form early in the day.

5. There are well defined busy periods in your work day.

Others needs specific to your situation:

6. _____
7. _____
8. _____
9. _____
10. _____

(See author's comments on page 86.)

> "Proper anticipation is the key to my day-to-day success. Without it, I'm out of business in no time."
> A Restaurant Manager

STEP II: IDENTIFY CUSTOMER NEEDS THROUGH YOUR . . .

ATTENTIVENESS

Attentiveness is the skill of understanding what your customers may need and want. It goes beyond timeliness and anticipation because it requires you to TUNE-IN to the HUMAN NEEDS of your customers.

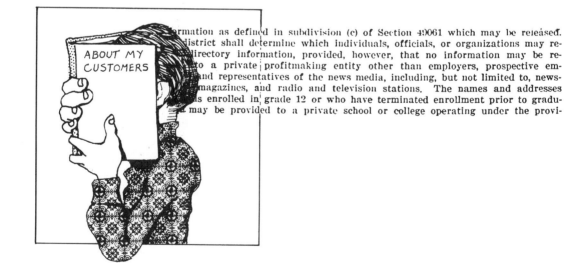

READING YOUR CUSTOMER

1. *READING THE CUSTOMER REQUIRES SENSITIVITY*.

   Reading the customer requires being sensitive to both nonverbal and verbal signals that customers send out (sometimes without being aware).

   Here are some common signals. Can you think of customer needs the following signals might be communicating?

Signal:		Possible Customer Need
Age of customer:	Young	_____
	Old	_____
Type of clothing:	High fashion	_____
	Out-of-fashion	_____
	Worn out	_____
Verbal ability:	Extremely fluent	_____
	Barely fluent	_____
Attitude:	Positive	_____
	Negative	_____
Impatient		_____
Demanding or angry		_____

   Compare your comments with those of the author on page 86.

2. *READING THE CUSTOMER REQUIRES EMPATHY*.

   Empathy is what *understanding* is all about. This means putting yourself in the position of your customers. You must view the situation through ''their eyes.'' You must ask, ''If I were this person, what would I want?''

   DO YOU HAVE THE ABILITY TO BE EMPATHETIC TO YOUR CUSTOMERS, CLIENTS OR GUESTS?

   _____ Yes   _____ No

   Why do you think so? _____

   _____

STEP II: IDENTIFY NEEDS BY . . .

UNDERSTANDING BASIC CUSTOMER NEEDS

Just like you, customers need . . .

help

respect

comfort

empathy

satisfaction

support

a friendly face

FOUR BASIC NEEDS

#1 *The Need to be Understood*

Those who select your service need to feel they are communicating effectively. This means the messages they send should be interpreted correctly. Emotions or language barriers can get in the way of proper understanding.

#2 *The Need to Feel Welcome*

Anyone doing business with you who feels like an outsider will not return. People need to feel you are happy to see them and that their business is important to you.

#3 *The Need to Feel Important*

Ego and self-esteem are powerful human needs. We all like to feel important. Anything you can do to make a guest feel special is a step in the right direction.

#4 *The Need for Comfort*

Customers need physical comfort; a place to wait, rest, talk, or do business. They also need psychological comfort; the assurance they will be taken care of properly, and the confidence you will meet their needs.

WHAT DO YOUR CUSTOMERS *DO* TO SIGNAL THESE NEEDS TO YOU?

The help you *identify* when your customers have one or more of these basic needs, indicate below what customers *do or say* that serve as a signal one or more needs requires your attention.

WHAT YOUR CUSTOMERS MIGHT DO OR SAY
TO SIGNAL A BASIC NEED: MESSAGE:

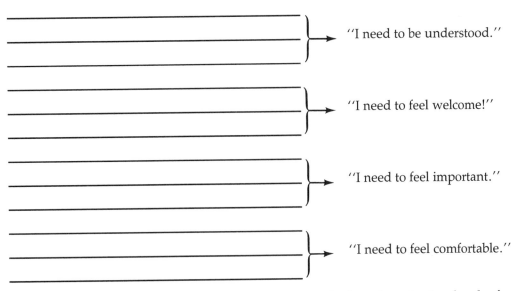

"I need to be understood."

"I need to feel welcome!"

"I need to feel important."

"I need to feel comfortable."

See the author's comments on what customers commonly do and say to signal each of these basic needs on page 86.

STEP II: IDENTIFY CUSTOMERS NEEDS BY . . .

SKILLFUL LISTENING

Five Ways to be a better listener:

1. Stop talking
2. Avoid distractions
3. Concentrate on what the other person is saying
4. Look for the "real" meaning
5. Provide feedback to the sender.

Lisa works in the reservations office of a hotel. She arrives early each morning to take reservations over the telephone. After each call, Lisa always repeats the day of arrival and number of nights of the reservation back to the caller and waits for confirmation. Her listening skills help keep mistakes at a minimum and customers happy.

"The most important activity any company can do is listen to its customers. Listen hard and listen well — that is the secret to financial success."

A Management Consultant

WHAT DO YOU KNOW ABOUT LISTENING SKILLS?

Ten faulty assumptions about listening are listed below. Read each carefully and check (✔) ones that you have previously held.

Don't forget to read carefully the correct assumptions about listening.

FAULTY ASSUMPTIONS	CORRECT ASSUMPTIONS
_____ 1. We learn to listen automatically; training is unnecessary.	Effective listening is a skill that is difficult for most of us. Practice and training can improve our ability to listen well.
_____ 2. Listening ability depends on intelligence.	There is no relationship between intelligence and listening skill.
_____ 3. Listening ability is closely related to hearing acuity.	Ability to hear is a physical phenomenon. It has little to do with our ability to listen. In fact, people with hearing loss often make extremely effective listeners.
_____ 4. Generally, most of us can listen well and read something else at the same time.	This is a skill few, if any, people can do effectively.
_____ 5. We listen well most of the time.	Unfortunately, most of us need to work on improving our listening skills.
_____ 6. What we hear is usually what was said.	As human beings, we have a natural tendency to filter information we hear. All too often, what we hear is not what was said.
_____ 7. Listening is a passive action.	Listening is an active process. It requires our *participation* and *involvement*.
_____ 8. Personality has little effect on listening ability.	Our personality plays an important role in how well we listen.
_____ 9. Listening is done only through the ears.	Effective listening is done with the whole body. Proper eye contact and body posture can facilitate effective listening.
_____10. Listening should be concerned with content first and feelings second.	Feelings are often more important than the words themselves. We must look for the underlying feelings in messages. They are often the REAL message.

STEP II: IDENTIFY NEEDS BY . . .

OBTAINING FEEDBACK

Do you know . . .

- What your customers want?
- What they need?
- What they think?
- How they feel?
- What suggestions they have?
- Whether they are satisfied?

Family-Fun Restaurant

A family-fun restaurant has initiated an aggressive program to solicit customer feedback. A dining room employee is assigned the task of personally asking guests at each table to fill out a feedback card. If the guests agree, the card is left at the table with a pencil. The guests deposit the card in a box at the front of the restaurant upon leaving. According to the restaurant's manager, several important improvements have been made in the operation as a result of customer suggestions. "This program has been invaluable," she states.

FEEDBACK

Every guest service operation should have ways to obtain feedback from customers. Several methods of finding out what your customers think and feel about the services you provide are listed below. Place a check (✔) by those feedback methods that are appropriate in your situation, and discuss any questions or ideas you have with your trainer/supervisor.

☐ Listening carefully to what customers/guests or clients have to say.

☐ Checking back regularly to see how things are going.

☐ Making feedback cards available for customers to comment on service.

☐ Providing a special phone number for guests, customers and/or clients to call for questions, problems or suggestions.

☐ Asking other employees to solicit regular feedback when appropriate.

☐ Insuring the manager has regular customer contact.

☐ Providing a method that invites customer criticism and responding constructively to any complaints.

☐ Acknowledging all positive comments and reactions as well as any negative ones.

☐ Other: _____

_____

☐ My ideas for improved feedback: _____

_____

QUESTION: What do a local hospital and an auto service department have in common?

ANSWER: They both use phone surveys to find out how satisfied their customers/patients are with the service they received.

STEP II:
SUMMARY AND FOLLOW-UP

SUMMARY

The best way to identify the needs of your customers is to try and put yourself in their position, see things from their perspective, put yourself in their shoes. This section of the book has outlined a number of suggestions to help you do this.

You can identify the needs of your customers by–

	I DO WELL	NEED IMPROVEMENT
• UNDERSTANDING THEIR HUMAN NEEDS	☐	☐
• KNOWING THEIR TIMING REQUIREMENTS	☐	☐
• ANTICIPATING THEIR NEEDS IN ADVANCE	☐	☐
• BEING ABLE TO "READ" YOUR CUSTOMERS	☐	☐
• UNDERSTANDING BASIC CUSTOMER NEEDS	☐	☐
• PRACTICING SKILLFUL LISTENING	☐	☐
• OBTAINING FEEDBACK	☐	☐

If at all possible, make a visit to your operation, or one just like it at another location, as a customer. Do every thing a customer would do. Make a *mental* note of what happens at the time and *afterwards* respond to the following questions:

1. What perspectives did you develop seeing your job from the other side of the fence?
2. How were you treated?
3. What went well?
4. What could have gone better?
5. What insights did you develop that will have a positive impact on how you perform your job?

STEP III:
PROVIDE FOR THE NEEDS OF YOUR GUESTS, CUSTOMERS OR CLIENTS

As an assistant manager in a large retail store, Joe was frustrated with the time and inconvenience of processing customers through the check out counters. When he finally became manager of his own store, Joe received permission from his district manager to experiment with a new check out system. The system was so successful, it was adopted throughout the entire chain and Joe received a well-deserved promotion.

WHAT SERVICES DO YOU PROVIDE?

The first step in providing quality customer service is to recognize and understand all the services that your organization wants to provide.

Describe below some of the services you will be providing. If you feel your response is incomplete, ask your trainer or supervisor for assistance.

Eight general categories of providing service are listed below. After each, write in specifically what YOU WILL DO to provide service in that particular area. Then, add any other services you provide that have not already been listed.

1. Receiving information for customers: _____

    _____

    _____

    _____

2. Providing information to customers: _____

    _____

    _____

    _____

3. Soliciting feedback from customers: _____

    _____

    _____

    _____

4. Following through on customers' requests: _____

    _____

    _____

    _____

5. Identifying and solving problems: _____

_____

_____

_____

6. Providing a service for customers: _____

_____

_____

_____

7. Watching or observing: _____

_____

_____

_____

8. Organizing: _____

_____

_____

_____

> ''Each of my major divisions is a service provider for the other divisions. For example, engineering must design parts that meet the needs of production. The production division must gear up to meet the orders from marketing. And the marketing division must keep engineering informed of changes in the marketplace. So you see, we all provide service to each other.''
>
> A Corporate CEO

WHAT ARE THE CHARACTERISTICS OF THE SERVICES YOU PROVIDE?

Understanding your SERVICE CHARACTERISTICS will allow you to appreciate how the services you provide are SEEN BY YOUR CUSTOMERS.

CONSIDER THESE TEN SERVICE CHARACTERISTICS:

1. People/Things Orientation.

Is the service you provide more people oriented or is it more oriented toward things (i.e., machines, equipment, and technology)?

2. High Tech/Low Tech.

If technology is involved in the delivery of the service provided, is it state-of-the-art, or are more traditional tools and/or systems used?

3. Personal Interaction.

This characteristic can be divided into three parts.

Physical: Do the parties involved in the service have to see each other? How close are they to each other? What type of touching is involved?

Mental: To what extent does the interaction demand the people involved to think, to analyze, to comprehend?

Emotional: To what extent does the interaction rely on emotional-based-reactions and/or situations?

4. Time Involvement.

How long (in duration) does the service take? How *frequently* does it occur?

5. Location.

Does the service take place at the customer's site, your locale, or somewhere else?

6. Complexity.

Actual: How complex is the service provided? How complicated are delivery systems?

Visual: How much complexity does the customer see? Do service delivery systems *appear* to be simple when they are really not?

7. Accommodation.

How flexible and adaptable are the service systems? To what extent can they be adjusted to meet unique or different customer needs or requests?

8. Numbers Served Per Transaction.

How many customers are provided service during a single service transaction? One or two? A small group? Hundreds? Thousands?

9. Training.

How much training, education, and/or expertise is needed to deliver service?

10. Supervision.

How much supervision does the service system require?

DEVELOP A SERVICE PROFILE

YOUR SERVICE PROFILE

CIRCLE THE RESPONSE THAT MOST CLOSELY MATCHES THE
NATURE OF THE SERVICE YOUR SERVICE TEAM PROVIDES.

1. People/Things Orientation	More Things	More People
2. Level of Technology	Hi Tech	Lo Tech
3. Personal Interaction: Physical	Hi	Lo
Mental	Hi	Lo
Emotional	Hi	Lo
4. Time Involvement: Duration	Long	Short
Frequency	Hi	Lo
5. Location	Their Place	Our Place
6. Complexity: Actual	Hi	Lo
Visual	Hi	Lo
7. Accommodation Ability	Hi	Lo
8. Numbers Served per Transaction	One	Many
9. Training required	Much	Little
10. Supervision needed	Much	Little

How does this service profile affect the type and level of service you can provide?

_____

_____

54

STEP III: PROVIDE QUALITY CUSTOMER SERVICE BY ...

PERFORMING IMPORTANT BACK-UP DUTIES

BACK-UP DUTIES

Treating customers special means performing back-up tasks with as much positive energy and interest as you demonstrate in other aspects of your job.

Often, back-up duties are shared with co-workers. Lending a hand, doing your fair share, pulling your weight...are all part of quality service.

When you are evaluated by your supervisor, you will probably be rated on how well you treat guests, PLUS, on how well you perform the back-up duties.

Common back-up duties include: stocking, filing, recording information, handling telephone calls, assisting with clean-up, running errands, and/or handling money.

WHAT ARE SOME OF THE BACK-UP TASKS YOU NORMALLY PERFORM?

LIST THE MAJOR ONES BELOW:

_____

_____

_____

_____

_____

_____

_____

_____

Check this list with your supervisor to see if you have forgotten anything critical to your job success.

| STEP III: | YOUR SUCCESS WILL DEPEND ON YOUR ABILITY TO . . . |

SEND
CLEAR
MESSAGES

Ralph runs a neighborhood bike shop. When hiring new employees for the busy fall season, he tries to tell them as much as he can about bicycles in one day. He does not spend time on training and always promises to write crucial information down, but never seems to find the time. Ralph can't understand why new employees take so long to learn the bicycle business. He laments, "I guess good help is hard to find these days."

PROMISES

The way in which you COMMUNICATE can *make* or *break* your success on the job!

| DO YOU KNOW HOW TO EFFECTIVELY SEND A MESSAGE? |

If you do, see if you can identify the true statements below.

____ 1. You should try to impress all customers about how knowledgeable you are.

____ 2. You should always strive to assure the self-esteem of your guest.

____ 3. Repeating the message back to the customer can help eliminate misunderstandings.

____ 4. Good eye contact with a guest is rarely important.

____ 5. When sending a message, it is important to use words that are easily understood.

____ 6. Silence on the part of a client or guest usually indicates understanding and acceptance of your message.

____ 7. The more you talk, the better you are at communicating.

____ 8. Effective communcation skills are inborn.

____ 9. Following up a verbal message with a written message can often facilitate effective communication.

____ 10. When coaching or helping a customer or fellow employee, you should focus on behavior, not on personality.

____ 11. Your tone of voice communicates as much, or more, of the message as the words themselves.

____ 12. Your body language sends direct messages to others regardless of what you are saying.

____ 13. Misunderstanding a customer request is really not a serious problem.

____ 14. Effective communication with guests or clients is more important than effective communication among fellow employees.

____ 15. Good employees keep their supervisors well-informed at all times.

| Answers: True statements are 2, 3, 5, 9, 10, 11, 12, and 15. |

"Keep your message short, sweet and to the point. Be specific. Choose the small word over a big one. Work on how to express, not how to impress."
A Communications Expert

QUALITY CUSTOMER SERVICE: Third Edition

| STEP III: | PROVIDE FOR CUSTOMER & GUEST NEEDS BY . . . |

SAYING THE RIGHT THING

A 275-pound man had just finished his dinner at a local steak house when the waiter walked up and said, "Boy, you made that steak disappear fast!" Later, the waiter couldn't understand why the customer complained to the manager.

SAYING THE RIGHT THING

In Step I of quality customer service, you used your physical appearance, body language and tone of voice to send a positive attitude.

Now, we must consider the ACTUAL WORDS to use in order to treat customers as guests.

Even though you have already communicated a great deal by your appearance and body language; it is important to complete your most effective communication skills by selecting the right words to say, and saying them in the right tone of voice.

In the space below write a "typical" script when you interact with customers while on the job. Include a greeting, the words you would say to handle your transaction, and the way you would conclude the session.

My greeting would be: _____

_____

I would handle the transaction by saying: _____

_____

_____

_____

_____

_____

_____

_____

Once the business had been taken care of, I would say: _____

_____

_____

REVIEW YOUR CHOICE OF WORDS WITH YOUR SUPERVISOR OR TRAINER.

STEP III: SATISFYING THE FOUR
BASIC NEEDS OF
YOUR CUSTOMERS BY . . .

- Showing understanding

- Making them feel welcome

- Helping them feel important

- Providing a comfortable environment

FOUR BASIC NEEDS

THE FOUR BASIC NEEDS OF CUSTOMERS

1. The need to be understood

2. The need to feel welcome

3. The need to feel important

4. The need for comfort

Your success on the job will depend on how well you and your organization PROVIDE for these four basic needs.

WHAT CAN YOU DO TO PROVIDE FOR THESE NEEDS?

Fill-in your thoughts and ideas on how to provide each of the four basic needs.

1) I plan to show *understanding* by _____

_____

_____

2) I plan to make my guests or customer *feel welcome* by _____

_____

_____

3) I plan to help my customer *feel important* by _____

_____

_____

4) I plan to provide a *comfortable environment* by

_____

_____

See author's comments on page 87.

STEP III: PRACTICE EXTENDING YOUR SERVICE BY ...

EFFECTIVELY SELLING

Your organization's unique products and/or services

Beth employs three agents at her travel agency. One agent, Mary Jeanne, books more flights, cruises and tours than the others combined. When asked the secret to her success, Mary Jeanne commented, "All I do is make my clients aware of the alternatives available to them. I try to be enthusiastic about each option, explaining what I think is important to that client. I also look for the deals. I want clients to feel they are getting exactly what they want for the lowest price possible. I always try to make them feel good about the plan they choose. They've got to like what they buy or they simply won't come back."

SELLING YOUR CUSTOMER AND/OR GUESTS ON THE QUALITY SERVICE YOU PROVIDE IS AN INTEGRAL PART OF YOUR JOB!

YOU SELL YOUR SERVICE BY:

1. Expanding AWARENESS of your available services.

2. Explaining the FEATURES of these services.

3. Describing the BENEFITS of these services.

Please list in the left-hand column below the major services you and your supervisor/trainer listed on page 50.

For each service you list in column (1), write a FEATURE or characteristic of that service in column (2), and how that service BENEFITS your customer and/or guests in column (3).

(1) SERVICES AVAILABLE*	(2) FEATURES of service	(3) BENEFITS of service

---

*The next time you mention these services remember to explain the FEATURES and BENEFITS. Your supervisor will be favorably impressed.

STEP III: AS TIME PASSES, MORE AND MORE EMPLOYEES WILL NEED TO LEARN HOW TO ...

MEET THE COMPUTER CHALLENGE

COMPUTER/CUSTOMER RELATIONS EXERCISE

An increasing number of jobs require you to meet the service needs of our customers through the use of a computer.

The computer (which is an object) requires your attention and skill, BUT NOT AT THE EXPENSE OF GUESTS AND/OR CUSTOMERS.

Five statements about computers and customer/client relations are presented below. Read each and indicate your "agreement" or "disagreement." Then, briefly explain the reasoning for your response.

STATEMENT   REASONING:

1. Operating a terminal at first may be so   Agree/   _____
   difficult that your ability to provide quality   Disagree   _____
   service is adversely affected.   Because: _____

2. Operating the computer properly is often   Agree/   _____
   more important than treating a customer as a   Disagree   _____
   guest.   Because: _____

3. When you have problems with the computer,
   the best thing to do is to devote absolute   Agree/   _____
   concentration in order to work out the   Disagree   _____
   problem.   Because: _____

4. Operating a computer terminal requires you   Agree/   _____
   to split concentration between it and a   Disagree   _____
   customer/guest.   Because: _____

5. If your transaction is long and involved, you
   should always let your customer know, and   Agree/   _____
   then compensate by being empathetic and   Disagree   _____
   friendly.   Because: _____

Compare your comments with those of the author on page 87.

PREPARE FOR THE UNEXPECTED

Everything doesn't always go as planned; a shipment is delayed, a key employee is ill, a newspaper ad carries an incorrect price. When the unexpected happens (and it will), the organization that is most concerned with customer service will usually come out ahead. The best approach is to think ahead to what might go wrong – and consider some back-up scenarios.

A California corporation has just initiated an earthquake preparedness program. Contingency plans have been fully developed for keeping services flowing in case the "big one" hits.

STEP III:	PROVIDING QUALITY CUSTOMER SERVICE MAY BE ESPECIALLY CHALLENGING WHEN–

THE UNEXPECTED HAPPENS

Unexpected occurrences often place extra burdens on your ability to deliver quality customer service. They may present a formidable challenge.

While all possible occurrences may not be foreseen, common or expected situations can be anticipated. In these cases, contingency plans can be developed to help you do your job under these possible abnormal circumstances.

A number of possible unexpected occurrences are listed below. Circle the ones that COULD POSSIBLY APPLY IN YOUR SITUATION and indicate any contingency action plans that could be followed to help maintain quality customer service. Discuss your ideas with your supervisor.

THE UNEXPECTED:

YOUR CONTINGENCY PLAN

1. Foul weather _____
2. Loss of power _____
3. Equipment failure _____
4. Computer breakdown _____
5. Overcrowded conditions _____
6. Understaffed _____
7. Fire/health emergency _____
8. Climate control malfunction _____
9. Phones out _____
10. Needed supplies exhausted _____
11. Breakdown in the delivery system _____
12. Other; you add: _____

STEP III: SUMMARY

You can provide for the needs of your customers by–

- Performing *all* the tasks and duties required of your job

- Performing important back-up duties

- Communicating by sending clear messages
    - –To customers,
    - –Supervisors, and
    - –Fellow employees

- Making only appropriate comments to customers

- Satisfying the four basic needs of your customers

- Practicing effective selling skills

- Meeting the computer challenge

- Continuing to deliver quality customer service when the unexpected occurs

STEP IV:
MAKE SURE YOUR CUSTOMERS, CLIENTS AND/OR GUESTS RETURN

Whether a customer purchases a complete wardrobe or a necktie, one medium-size department store makes it a policy to follow-up each sale with a brief thank you note. The president of the company says, "Such a policy encourages customers to return, and that's what makes our business thrive."

WHAT YOU CAN DO TO MAKE SURE CUSTOMERS COME BACK

On the facing page is a list of items you can do personally to make sure that customers return.

Some interesting statistics* tell why companies lose customers:

1% of lost customers die.
3% move away.
4% just naturally float.
5% change on friend's recommendations.
9% can buy it cheaper somewhere else.
10% are chronic complainers.
68% go elsewhere because the people they deal with are indifferent to their needs.

Customers are not the frosting on the cake—*they are the cake.* The frosting is an improved reputation and higher profits as a result of a quality job.

IMPORTANT PAGE!

---

*Reprinted from *QUALITY AT WORK*. To order this excellent 50-Minute book on personal standards of quality, contact Crisp Publications, Inc. at 1-800-442-7477.

MAKING SURE CUSTOMERS RETURN

Rank those items that apply to your job and then ask your supervisor to do the same. Compare the responses and discuss any differences.

YOUR RANKINGS		YOUR SUPERVISOR'S RANKINGS
_____	1. Always be pleasant to customers even if they are not pleasant to you.	_____
_____	2. Welcome customer/guest suggestions about how you could improve in your job.	_____
_____	3. Graciously receive and handle any complaints or problems.	_____
_____	4. Go "above and beyond" to care for a customer.	_____
_____	5. Smile even during those times when you don't feel like it.	_____
_____	6. Roll with the punches, accepting bad news or harried schedules calmly.	_____
_____	7. Provide service that is beyond what customers expect from you.	_____
_____	8. Provide helpful suggestions and/or guidance when you feel customers need it.	_____
_____	9. Thoroughly explain the features and benefits for all of the services you provide.	_____
_____	10. Follow through to ensure your customer commitments are honored.	_____

STATISTICS SAY IT COSTS SIX TIMES MORE TO ATTRACT A NEW CUSTOMER THAN KEEP A CURRENT ONE.

STEP IV: MAKE SURE CUSTOMERS RETURN BY . . .

DOING WHAT YOU CAN TO SATISFY THOSE WHO COMPLAIN

Miss Johnson:
Please explain
to these nice people
how they all ended up
in suite 124.

HANDLING COMPLAINTS

Steps You Should Take

1. LISTEN carefully to the complaint
2. REPEAT the complaint back and get acknowledgement you heard it correctly
3. APOLOGIZE
4. ACKNOWLEDGE the customer or guest's feelings (anger, frustration, disappointment, etc.)
5. EXPLAIN what action you will take to correct the problem
6. THANK the customer for bringing the problem to your attention

Situation — FRONT DESK

A guest approaches the front desk of your hotel and is visibly upset. He informs you that the room you just assigned him, is ''uninhabitable'' because it smells strongly of cigarette smoke. Neither he nor his wife smoke and the odor is making them nauseated. He informs you that he feels a hotel of this caliber and price should have no smoking rooms. He demands immediate action.

WHAT WOULD YOU SAY TO THIS GUEST?

Record your action plan below:

ACTION

Repeat the complaint: _____

_____

Apologize: _____

Acknowledge the feelings: _____

_____

Explain what you will do: _____

_____

Thank the guest: _____

_____

See author comments on page 87.

COMMON COMPLAINTS

Most customer service operations often find that customers tend to complain about some things more than others.

DO YOU KNOW WHAT THESE MOST COMMON COMPLAINTS ARE?

DO YOU KNOW WHAT *TO DO* AND *WHAT TO SAY* WHEN YOU ARE FACED WITH ONE?

Talk with your supervisor before you fill this out.

Use the left-hand column below to list the most common customer complaints you can anticipate facing on your job.

For each complaint you list on the left, indicate, on the right, how you should handle the complaint. This includes (1) what you would do and (2) what you would say.

COMMON COMPLAINTS: **RECOMMENDED ACTION:**

_____   _____

_____   _____

_____   _____

_____   _____

_____   _____

_____   _____

TYPES OF DIFFICULT CUSTOMERS
WHOM YOU MAY HAVE TO DEAL WITH:

- the angry customer
- the nasty or obnoxious person
- the seething, but silent individual
- the demanding client
- the constant critic

- the nonstop talker
- the oddball
- the indecisive person
- the intoxicated guest
- the argumentative patient

Your addition: _____

_____

WHY ARE THESE PEOPLE DIFFICULT?

Most difficult people are operating from a base of INSECURITY. Like all of us, they too, have a need to be understood, feel welcome, comfortable and important.

Difficult people are often merely expressing a need; although they are choosing an inappropriate and impolite way to communicate this need.

THEY ARE BEING DIFFICULT FOR THEIR OWN REASONS —
NOT BECAUSE OF YOU.

Here are some common reasons why customers may be difficult. Check the ones that may apply to you and your situation.

_____ 1. They are tired or frustrated.

_____ 2. They are confused or overwhelmed.

_____ 3. They are defending their ego or self-esteem.

_____ 4. They have never been in a similar situation before.

_____ 5. They feel ignored. Nobody has listened to them.

_____ 6. They may be under the influence of alcohol or drugs.

_____ 7. They don't speak or understand the language very well.

_____ 8. They have been treated poorly in similar circumstances in the past.

_____ 9. They are in a bad mood and take it out on you.

_____ 10. They are in a hurry or have waited an extended period of time for service.

_____ 11. Other; you specify _____

_____

STEP IV: MAKE SURE CUSTOMERS RETURN BY . . .

LEARNING TO GET DIFFICULT CUSTOMERS ON YOUR SIDE

STEP ONE: **Don't take it personally.**
This is one of the hardest customer-service skills to learn. Remember, they are not attacking you personally (even though it may seem that they are).

STEP TWO: **Remain calm. Listen carefully.**
This is easy to say here, but difficult to do. Take a deep breath and plan your words carefully. Paraphrase what they have said to make sure you have heard them correctly.

STEP THREE: **Focus on the problem, not the person.**
Go to a quiet area. Sit down. Be a problem solver. Try to figure out what this person needs and satisfy this need in some way, if you can. Let them know what you CAN DO.

STEP FOUR: **Reward yourself for turning a difficult customer into a happy one.**

CASE #2
THE DIFFICULT CUSTOMER

Situation — Airline Ticket Counter

A middle-aged woman approaches the ticket counter of an airline at a large airport and demands to see the manager. You ask if you can be of any assistance since the manager is not available. She immediately challenges the airline's no pet policy as unfair and discriminatory. She explains that she has to travel 1000 miles to attend a sick sister. Her toy poodle, with whom she has never been separated, is completely house broken and "never barks or bites." She can't stand the thought of her "little baby" all alone in the dangerous, cold and dark baggage compartment. After all, "dogs can freeze up there and there may not be enough air to breathe." She is holding the dog tightly in her arms. The pooch is clothed in a designer jacket made for small dogs and has her nails polished bright red. The lady loudly demands she be allowed to bring her pet on board with her.

WHAT SHOULD YOU DO? Place an (x) in the box of the actions below that are the most appropriate response to this difficult situation:

- [ ] 1. Show slight disgust on your face so she will know you consider *her* to be the problem.
- [ ] 2. Laugh and make light of the situation.
- [ ] 3. Remain calm, cool and patient.
- [ ] 4. Sympathize with her feelings of fear and frustration. Tell her that you don't like to leave your pets alone either.
- [ ] 5. Walk away to find the manager.
- [ ] 6. Become distant and less cooperative.
- [ ] 7. Disarm her by asking, "Are you serious?"
- [ ] 8. Explain carefully about the gentle treatment pets receive in the pet compartment and how many pets fly your airline each day.
- [ ] 9. Ask her to understand the airline's need to consider all the passengers.
- [ ] 10. Thank her for understanding and cooperating.

See comments of author on page 87.

> WHEN YOU FIND YOURSELF CONFRONTED WITH A DIFFICULT SITUATION YOU DON'T KNOW HOW TO HANDLE, INVOLVE YOUR SUPERVISOR.
>
> CERTAIN PROBLEMS MAY REQUIRE YOUR SUPERVISOR TO HANDLE THEM. IF SO, FIND OUT WHAT THESE PROBLEM AREAS ARE, AND OBSERVE HOW THEY ARE HANDLED.

STEP IV: MAKE SURE CUSTOMERS WILL RETURN BY . . .

TAKING THAT ONE EXTRA SERVICE STEP

Patty, a part-time employee in a neighborhood gift shop, was helping a young woman in a hurry. While the woman was looking for the right card, Patty was wrapping the gift to which the card would be attached. Suddenly Patty realized that the customer was taking the gift directly with her and said, "I'll bet you will need a pen to sign the card. Here, take this one with you." The customer said in surprise, "Yes. How did you know? Thank you very much."

SURPRISE YOUR CUSTOMERS! TREAT THEM AS GUESTS! GO BEYOND WHAT THEY EXPECT!

Examples:

Ticket Agent:	"Would you like me to select a seat for your return flight at this time?"
Salesperson:	"I'll deliver it personally this afternoon."
Night nurse:	"Since you are awake, let me find some ginger-ale for you to drink."
Loan officer:	"I don't know the answer now, but I'll call you back before 11:00 a.m. with the answer."
Waitress:	"May I bring an extra plate so you can share our special dessert?"
Hotel desk clerk:	"May I call a cab for you?"
Auto mechanic:	"Since your car will be longer than planned, may I give you a lift home?"
Receptionist in a state agency:	"To avoid getting lost on the third floor, let me draw a map for you."
Grocery clerk:	"Let me get you some help carrying out your groceries."
Bank clerk:	"Take this new checkbook cover. Yours looks a little worn."

HOW CAN *YOU* TAKE THAT EXTRA STEP OF SERVICE?

List ways you feel would be appropriate for your job. Then, share the list with your supervisor for his/her reaction.

1. _____
2. _____
3. _____
4. _____
5. _____
6. _____
7. _____
8. _____
9. _____
10. _____

STEP IV: SUMMARY

Make sure your customers, clients and/or guests return by—

- Working to satisfy customer complaints

- Being prepared to properly handle the most common complaints

- Learning to get difficult customers on your side

- Understanding why some customers are more difficult than others

- Taking that one extra step to provide quality customer service

- Consistently practicing *all* the principles of quality customer service that you have learned about in this book

P A R T

III

Notes and Comments

CHECK YOUR PROGRESS

TRUE OR FALSE

_____ 1. People who are successful at customer relations constantly need to be the center of attention.

_____ 2. Treating customers as guests means viewing your job primarily as a human relations representative.

_____ 3. Guest service employees are at the mercy of their customers, and thus, have little control over their success on the job.

_____ 4. Treating customers as guests often means apologizing for mistakes you did not make.

_____ 5. It really isn't important to remember the names and faces of your customers.

_____ 6. If you have limited desire to please others, you probably shouldn't be in a service related job.

_____ 7. How you handle the procedural (or technical) side of your job can directly affect how you handle the personal side.

_____ 8. Knowing the time requirements for providing quality service will help you do a better job.

_____ 9. Good anticipation means providing items and services for customers without requiring them to ask.

_____ 10. When communicating with another person, it is important to always consider and protect his or her self esteem.

_____ 11. Eye contact has little impact on good communication.

_____ 12. Feedback rarely provides the information necessary to do a better job.

_____ 13. If you are not careful, working on a computer can adversely affect your attentiveness toward customers/guests.

_____ 14. Generally, the attitude you receive from others is the same attitude you transmit.

_____ 15. Reading the customer correctly can pay great dividends for you and your organization.

_____ 16. Most people simply want fast service and have little need to feel important or be recognized.

_____ 17. Body language often communicates more than the actual words you use.

_____ 18. When a guest is rude, obnoxious and impolite, it is justifiable for you to return the same behavior.

_____ 19. It is really impractical to think that you should try to go one step beyond the expectations of those you serve.

_____ 20. Customer complaints should be encouraged.

ANSWERS ON PAGE 87.

FOLLOW-UP

You have now completed this program. This is
an excellent time to sit down with your manager
and/or trainer and talk about what you have
learned. This is also a good time to clarify any
questions you may have about the job.

TELL YOUR MANAGER YOU HAVE COMPLETED THE
PROGRAM AND ARRANGE A MEETING!

Use the space below to make notes about what
you want to talk about or questions you still have.

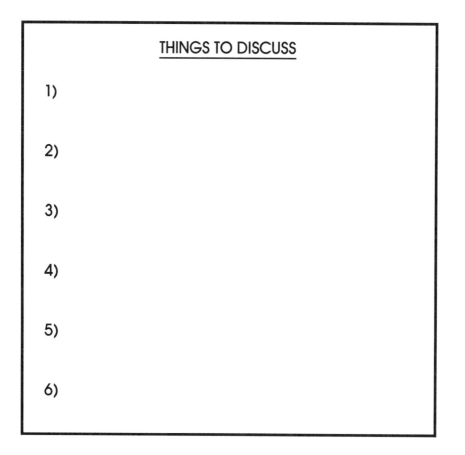

THINGS TO DISCUSS

1)

2)

3)

4)

5)

6)

AUTHOR'S NOTES AND COMMENTS

Body Language Exercise (p. 23)

Positive Messages:

Face is relaxed and under control. This communicates you are prepared, know what you are doing, and/or are comfortable with your role.

Smile is natural and comfortable. This communicates you are sure of yourself, like what you are doing and enjoy your guests.

Eye contact is maintained when talking and listening with guests. This communicates guests are important, you are interested in them and are self-confident.

Body movement is deliberate and controlled. This communicates you are in control, you are glad to be where you are and that although busy that's just part of the job.

Negative Messages:

Face is anxious and uptight. This communicates you are ill prepared, inexperienced and/or uncomfortable with your role.

Smile is forced or phony. This communicates you are unsure of yourself, don't like what you are doing, and/or really don't enjoy your guests.

Eye contact is avoided when talking and listening to customers. This communicates a lack of interest in guest, and/or you lack the self-confidence to do the job.

Body movement is harried and rushed. This communicates you are not in control of the situation, and would really like the guests to leave.

Listening to the Sound of Your Own Voice (p. 25)

The tone of voice that is conducive to your success in customer relations can be described by any of these four characteristics:
1. It is upbeat.
2. It is warm, comfortable and understanding.
3. It is under control.
4. It is clear, direct and natural.

CASE: Thelma's Performance Appraisal (p. 31)

Is Thelma a good employee? The answer is both "yes" and "no." She certainly does half of her job well — the non-people side. When it comes to interacting with customers, a very important part of the job, Thelma is not a good employee.

Is the manager justified in his recommendations? Answer: I think so. He cannot afford someone like Thelma turning off customers. His business relies on warm, friendly customer relations.

What recommendations would you make to Thelma? Answer: Learn and practice the principles of quality customer service as soon as possible or seek a position in the restaurant or elsewhere that won't require customer interaction.

Timeliness (p. 37)

The value of this exercise is to establish clear timeliness expectations between you and your supervisor or trainer. You may have your own ideas of what is timely, but it is more important to find out what your supervisor considers to be timely. In fact, your job may depend upon it.

AUTHOR'S NOTES AND COMMENTS (continued)

Anticipate Customer Needs (p. 39)

Situation:	Anticipated Need:
A customer has waited longer than usual for service.	An extra warm smile. A verbal recognition of the extended wait. A comment of appreciation for waiting. Speedy service.
A client is looking at his watch.	This person may have a plane to catch or another appointment. Recognize this need and provide timely service.
A woman guest with three small children.	Provide some items to occupy the children while they wait.
Lines for service form early.	Have appropriate supplies and equipment on hand. Have enough staff to meet the demand.
You have well-defined busy periods.	Prepare yourself mentally and physically. Don't be caught off guard.

Reading the Customer Exercise (p. 41)

Young:		Some young customers may be inexperienced or unsure of themselves. Explain things clearly. Be patient and set them at ease.
Old:		Seniors appreciate a friendly comment or two. Make casual conversation. Show some interest and attention.
Type of clothing:	High fashion:	Show well-dressed people the respect and deference they expect.
	Out-of-fashion:	Help these people feel welcome and comfortable.
Verbal ability:	Extremely fluent:	Listen carefully. Paraphrase back what you hear.
	Barely fluent:	Listen carefully. Explain things simply and clearly.
Attitude:	Positive:	Recognize and encourage it.
	Negative:	Be positive and understanding. Show empathy.
Impatient:		Be as timely as you can be. Explain what's happening. Explain how long the process will take. Be polite.
Demanding or angry:		Be polite and patient. Listen carefully. Stay calm. Show understanding.

Four Basic Needs (p. 43)

Customers express these four needs in a variety of ways. Here are just a few of them.

1) The Need to be Understood. This need is signaled by customers repeating themselves; speaking slowly; speaking loudly; getting angry when they are not being understood, or bringing a friend or relative to help explain.

2) The Need to Feel Welcome. This need is signaled by "looking around" before coming in and/or coming in with friends or relatives. It is also demonstrated by wearing the "right" clothes for the situation.

3) The Need to Feel Important. This need is often signaled by someone "showing off' or bragging about who they know. This need is also demonstrated by flashing money, a display of jewelry and/or extreme clothing.

4) The Need for Comfort. This need is expressed by customers being ill at ease, nervous, or unsure of themselves when feeling uncomfortable. This need is also expressed when help, assistance or directions are requested.

AUTHOR'S NOTES AND COMMENTS (continued)

<u>Satisfying Basic Customer Needs</u> (p. 61)

1) Need to be Understood:	Paraphrase back what is being said. Listen for feelings communicated as well as the content of the message. Empathize with problems or predicaments.
2) Need to Feel Welcome:	Provide a warm and friendly welcome. Talk in a language everyone will understand. Engage in friendly conversation.
3) Need to Feel Important:	Learn to call others by name. Do something special. Tune-in to individual needs.
4) Need for Comfort:	Set customers at ease. Relieve anxiety. Explain the service procedures carefully and calmly.

<u>Computer/Customer Relations Exercise</u> (p. 65)

1. Agree: You may sacrifice valuable customer time getting the computer to work properly. If you can practice on the computer before hours or during slow periods, this problem should be minimized.
2. Disagree: You must learn to treat customers as guests *and* operate the computer properly. Both are vital to your job success.
3. Disagree: Never concentrate on a computer problem *at the expense of a customer.* Get some assistance right away.
4. Agree: This is true; however, operating the computer soon becomes second nature. When this happens, you will be able to focus the majority of your attention on the customers.
5. Agree: Always let your client know what is going on. Sometimes a wait or delay doesn't seem quite as long when you have received an explanation for the delay.

<u>Handling Complaints</u> (p. 73)

A possible dialogue might go something like this:
"Your room smells strongly of cigarette smoke." (Repeating the complaint). "I'm very sorry, sir." (Apology). "You certainly have a right to be upset. I would be too." (Acknowledgement of feelings). "What I would like to do, if it is okay with you, is move you and your wife to another room right away. I'll have a bellman assist you." (Explaining the action that you will take). "Would that be all right?"
Guest: "Much better."
"Thank you for bringing this to my attention. I'm glad you told me about it. It should not have happened." (Thanking the guest).

<u>The Difficult Customer</u> (p. 77)

The correct responses to this situation would be to —
3 Remain calm, cool and patient.
4 Recognize the feelings of frustration and fear she expressed by telling her that you don't like to leave your pets alone either.
8 Tell her about the gentle treatment pets receive in the pet compartment and how many pets fly your airline each day.
#10 Thank her for understanding and cooperating.

<u>Review True-False Test</u> (p. 83)

1. F (Treating customers as guests means to make them the center of attention.) 2. T 3. F (You have almost complete control over your job success.) 4. T 5. F (Remembering names and faces is one of the most important things you can do.) 6. T 7. T 8. T 9. T 10. T 11. F (Eye contact has a great impact on communication.) 12. F (Member feedback provides invaluable information.) 13. T 14. T 15. T 16. F (Most members want to be served quickly and efficiently AND need to feel important and recognized.) 17. T 18. F (It is never justifiable to be rude or short with a guest.) 19. F (Going one step beyond the expectations of your guests should become a natural extension of your job.) 20. T.

TO THE SUPERVISOR AND/OR TRAINER

Quality Customer Service has been designed to make your job as trainer more effective, and, hopefully a bit easier. This book is NOT intended to replace on-the-job training. Its purpose is to set the stage for more efficient hands-on training.

Flexibility
This book breaks the art of treating customers as guests into four simple steps: 1) transmitting a positive attitude, 2) identifying customer needs, 3) providing for customer needs, and 4) cultivating repeat business. Ideally the trainee will complete each step BEFORE actual customer contact, although these learning steps can be used effectively at any time.

If you are using *Quality Customer Service* to compliment other training that is taking place, each step may be assigned independently or in concert with other sessions. The program is highly adaptable and can be used with most training programs.

Feedback and Discussion
Trainees will want to discuss the exercises in the book. Questions will arise that only you can answer. The following sections in the book suggest your involvement.

I.   A discussion of the case, "Thelma's Performance Appraisal," (page 31) is helpful and will serve as a general review of Step I.
II. The "Timeliness" exercise on page 37 asks for your input based on the specific timing requirements of your organization.
III. The trainee may need help listing all of the services he/she will be providing as well as services provided by others on page 50. You may also want to review the trainee's script for handling a customer transaction on page 59.
IV. Following pages 73 and 74 you may wish to discuss the policies and procedures you may have for handling customer complaints or difficult guests.

Upon Completion of the Program
A follow-up session between you and the trainee is suggested at the end of the program. To make the session most effective, you should arrange a meeting and discuss each section of the book. The feedback that follows should help you establish a supportive relationship with your employee. The time you devote to these sessions will be well invested.

NOTE:
The author of this book has written a similar work for supervisors and/or trainers titled *Managing Quality Customer Service*. It is also in the 50-Minute Series and filled with helpful tips, examples and worksheets aimed at those responsible for managing a quality program.

For more information on this book call Crisp Publications, Inc. at 1-800-442-7477.

NOTES

FOR OTHER FIFTY-MINUTE SELF-STUDY BOOKS
SEE THE BACK OF THIS BOOK.

NOTES

We hope you enjoyed this book. If so, we have good news for you. This title is part of the best-selling *FIFTY-MINUTE*™ *Series* of books. All *Series* books are similar in size and identical in price. Several are supported with training videos (identified by the symbol ⓥ next to the title).

FIFTY-MINUTE Books and Videos are available from your distributor. A free catalog is available upon request from Crisp Publications, Inc., 1200 Hamilton Court, Menlo Park, California 94025.

FIFTY-MINUTE Series Books & Videos organized by general subject area.

Management Training:

ⓥ	Coaching & Counseling	68-8
	Conducting Training Sessions	193-7
	Delegating for Results	008-6
	Developing Instructional Design	076-0
ⓥ	Effective Meeting Skills	33-5
ⓥ	Empowerment	096-5
	Ethics in Business	69-6
	Goals & Goal Setting	183-X
	Handling the Difficult Employee	179-1
ⓥ	An Honest Day's Work: Motivating Employees	39-4
ⓥ	Increasing Employee Productivity	10-8
ⓥ	Leadership Skills for Women	62-9
	Learning to Lead	43-4
ⓥ	Managing Disagreement Constructively	41-6
ⓥ	Managing for Commitment	099-X
	Managing the Older Work Force	182-1
ⓥ	Managing Organizational Change	80-7
	Managing the Technical Employee	177-5
	Mentoring	123-6
ⓥ	The New Supervisor—Revised	120-1
	Personal Performance Contracts—Revised	12-2
ⓥ	Project Management	75-0
ⓥ	Quality at Work: A Personal Guide to Professional Standards	72-6
	Rate Your Skills As a Manager	101-5
	Recruiting Volunteers: A Guide for Nonprofits	141-4
	Risk Taking	076-9
	Selecting & Working with Consultants	87-4
	Self-Managing Teams	00-0
	Successful Negotiation—Revised	09-2
	Systematic Problem Solving & Decision Making	63-7

Management Training (continued):

Personal Improvement:

Human Resources & Wellness:

Human Resources & Wellness (continued):

Communications & Creativity:

Customer Service/Sales Training:

Small Business & Financial Planning:

Adult Literacy & Learning:

Career/Retirement & Life Planning: